Hummingbirds

Curious Kids Press

Please note:All Rights Reserved. No part of this publication may be reproduced in any form or by any means, including scanning, photocopying, or otherwise without prior written permission of the copyright holder. Copyright © 2014

Hummingbirds

There are 320 species of the Hummingbird. They are among the smallest species of birds in the world. They get their name from the "humming" sound their wings make. Hummingbirds can be spotted in backyards and gardens in the summer months. Let's explore some more fun facts about this interesting bird. In this book we will discover what these birds eat, how they nest and many other fascinating facts. Read on to be amazed...

Where in the World?

Did you know the hummingbird likes the warm climates? Hummingbirds are found only in the Western Hemisphere. This is from southeastern Alaska to southern Chile, but most of them live in the tropics. Out of all the species of hummingbirds only 12 species spend the summer in North America, then migrate to warmer weather for the winter.

The Body of a Hummingbird

Did you know the hummingbird has colorful feathers? In the sunlight, the feathers of this bird are iridescent (change color). Hummingbirds can grow up to 8 inches long (20 centimeters). They do not weigh very much. The biggest ones only weigh about 7 ounces.

The Wings of a Hummingbird

Did you know the wings of this tiny bird move very fast? The hummingbird can flap its wings up to 200 times-per-second. It can also fly right, left, up, down, backwards and even upside down. Plus, this bird is also able to hover by flapping its wings in a figure-8 pattern.

The Hummingbird's Tongue

Did you know the hummingbird's tongue is super-long? It uses this long tongue to drink nectar from the center of long, tubular flowers. When the hummingbird finds a tasty flower it will stick its long, tapered bill into the center of it. From here it can lick the food at a rate of 13 licks-per-second.

What a Hummingbird Eats

Did you know the hummingbird eats more than just nectar? Hummingbirds mostly dine on flower nectar, tree sap, insects and pollen. This little bird must eat an enormous amount of food each day. This is because it has a very high body temperature, a super-fast heartbeat and fast breathing.

The Hummingbird's Special Ability

Did you know some species of the hummingbird make long journeys? Hummingbirds that are found in Canada and some parts of the US, must migrate for the winter. This means the hummingbird will fly from these cold areas to warmer ones. Most of these hummingbirds will go to Mexico, then begin the journey back in the springtime.

The Hummingbird as Prey

Did you know even though this bird is small and quick it still has predators? Animals like cats, snakes, lizards, larger birds and even frogs and preying mantis may catch and eat a hummingbird. Loss of habitat has also endangered this bird, so it is important to keep lots of flowers in your backyard gardens to help it out.

Hummingbird Communication

Did you know hummingbirds can communicate with visual displays? An angry hummingbird will defend its territory. It has been seen chasing larger birds, other hummingbirds and even people. It will dive at the offender, then zoom off quickly.

The Hummingbird Nest

Did you know the mother hummingbird will find a safe location to build her nest? She looks for an area that is sheltered from the wind, rain and too much sunlight. She may choose to make her tiny nest in the fork of two thin branches. She will use materials like, moss, dandelions or cattails, small bits of bark or leaves, as well as feathers and spider silk.

The Mom Hummingbird

Did you know mom hummingbird can lay from 1 to 3 eggs? She will sit on her eggs for about 20 days. When the baby birds hatch out, the mother bird tends to them. She feeds them insects and nectar. Mom hummingbird does this by sticking her long bill down her babies throats.

Baby Hummingbirds

Did you know baby hummingbirds grow very fast? In fact, the young start to fly in 18 to 30 days. Baby hummingbirds are very tiny when they are born. As they grow the nest will expand with them. This is because the mother has used spider silk in it, so it is very stretchy.

Life of a Hummingbird

Did you know a healthy hummingbird can live a long time? Some species of this bird can live longer than 10 years. The first year of a hummingbird's life is the hardest. To help hummingbirds, plant red, yellow or pink tubular flowers in your garden. These are its favorite.

The Bee Hummingbird

Did you know this is the smallest hummingbird species? This little creature only measures about 2.4 inches long (6 centimeters). It weighs about as much as a penny does. This hummingbird lives in Cuba and has very pretty feathers.

The Ruby-throated Hummingbird

Did you know this species of hummingbird migrates? It is known for the beautiful ruby-red coloring on it neck and throat area. The rest of its body is iridescent green. It has very tiny legs, so it cannot hop or walk very well. It measures about 3.5 inches long (9 centimeters).

The Giant Hummingbird

Did you know this is the biggest hummingbird of them all? It has a wingspan of 8.5 inches wide (21.5 centimeters). However, being bigger does slow it down. It can only flap its wings at 12 flaps-per-second. This big guy can be found in South America.

Quiz

Question 1: How many species of hummingbird are there?

Answer 1: 320

Question 2: What is special about the hummingbird's wings?

Answer 2: They can beat super-fast and move the bird in all directions

Question 3: Where does the mother hummingbird build her nest?

Answer 3: In a safe location protected from the wind, rain and too much sunlight

Question 4: At what age can baby hummingbirds fly?

Answer 4: 18 to 30 days

Question 5: What hummingbird weighs the same as a penny?

Answer 5: The Bee Hummingbird

Thank you for checking out another title from Curious Kids Press! Make sure to search "Curious Kids Press" on Amazon.com for many other great books.

CPSIA information can be obtained
at www.ICGtesting.com
Printed in the USA
LVIC06n2257071215
465870LV00016B/112

ISBN 9781500306472